LOVE LETTERS
TO THE SOUL

ALANA GRAINGER

Queensland, Australia

Copyright © 2025 by **Alana Grainger**

All rights reserved. Apart from fair dealing for the purposes of study, research, criticism or review as permitted under the Copyright Act, no part of this publication may be reproduced, distributed or transmitted in any form or by any means without prior written permission.

Please be aware that this novel has been written in Australian English and uses Australian language, spelling, grammar and punctuation conventions. These are notably different to American, Canadian and British language conventions.

The Vesica Piscis is a sacred symbol rich in geometric and spiritual significance – a portal for the non-physical to become known in the physical realm.

Cover design by Judith San Nicolas
Typeset: Garamond 12 pt/English157BT 28 pt/Cormorant Garamond 20 pt
Printed and bound in Australia by IngramSpark
Prepared for publication by The Erudite Pen: theeruditepen.com

 A catalogue record for this book is available from the National Library of Australia

Love Letters to the Soul – Alana Grainger 1st ed.
ISBN 9781764115100
eISBN 9781764115117

You have to grow from the inside out.
None can teach you, none can make you spiritual.
There is no other teacher but your own Soul.
Swami Vivekananada

Read slowly…

Spirit, as referred to in this text, is the awareness of a greater union of harmonious collective energy.

Soul is the unique and individualised aspect of one's own being that is a manifestation of Spirit Itself.

Contents

Preface 1
Introduction to the Love Letters 5
Love Letter One Searching For You 9
Love Letter Two Revelations of Separation 15
Love Letter Three The Fall 19
Love Letter Four The Pledge 23
Love Letter Five Turning Inwards 27
Love Letter Six Sacred Union 31
Love Letter Seven It Will Not Be the Last 35
Love Letter Eight Poised and Ready 39
Love Letter Nine The Power of 'Yes' 43
Love Letter Ten The Ring Master 47
Love Letter Eleven Baptism of Truth 49
Love Letter Twelve Divine Timing 53
Love Letter Thirteen The Silent Echo 57
Love Letter Fourteen Confronting Vulnerability ... 61
Love Letter Fifteen Follow the Energy 65
Love Letter Sixteen In Devotion to You 69
Love Letter Seventeen The Unbecoming 73
Love Letter Eighteen Honouring Cycles 77
Love Letter Nineteen Soul Grows Character 81

Love Letter Twenty The Shadowlands 85

Love Letter Twenty-one Accountability 89

Love Letter Twenty-two A Play of Shadow & Light. 93

Love Letter Twenty-three Overcoming Resistance 97

Love Letter Twenty-four The True Depth of Love ... 103

Love Letter Twenty-five Receptivity 107

Love Letter Twenty-six The Return 111

Love Letter Twenty-seven Integration 115

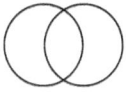

Preface

I had moved to Bali on a whim a year before I wrote these letters, chasing the dream that relocating would somehow realign my life so that I could embody the glamorous, yoga-vibe, freedom seeking, bohemian lifestyle that the island flamboyantly advertises as having.

Yet the longer I was there, the more my life as I knew it began to unravel. What had always been important to me no longer was, and the seemingly irrelevant and trivial aspects of my life loomed larger, holding greater weight. What did I want to do with this life? Who was I really? How could I authentically share from a place of integrity without letting my ego run the show? Do I have the capacity to be unashamedly myself? Can I find the courage to be vulnerable and let people see the real me? What would I be willing to sacrifice to bring forth this truth?

Having spent several extended expeditions traversing India, I believed I was more than prepared for what Bali could throw at me. India, I can see now from a place of hindsight, was the preliminary stage. It had peeled back layers, stripping me of the idea of who I thought I was so that I began to question myself and the existence of life. I'd faced fears; encountered the darker aspects of my being and stared them down; lovingly welcoming them into my fold; traversed a dark night of the soul; looked and (presumptuously and prematurely) 'healed' myself; had numerous mystical encounters; and on several occasion felt that I had stepped momentarily into a world beyond form.

Bali then, I surmised, would be the piece de resistance, the place where I graduated into the new evolved, radiant and resilient being who was ready to take on the world and live that idyllic dream life. Foolishly, I under estimated Bali's intensity for purification and transformation. It is widely known in circles in Bali that the island will only permit you to stay as long as She deems fit. When you're done, you're done, and you will know when that time is. Ignore those subtle hints at your own peril.

As a ticket to ride her wild, unfathomable and unstoppable wave, I had bought my 'in' via a Yoga Teacher Training. I later came to see this investment as a donation, an offering, a piece of myself given to the island in devotion. Unbeknown to me, this signalled the beginning of the de-scent as the conch shell (Shankha) had been blown. For what goes up in spirit must come down to be embodied in form. Unceremoniously, I was dragged down into my own hell. I encountered death after death of self and when I thought there was nothing left, still I descended further as I clung to every last piece of me that was being obliterated. I thought I had dissolved what had overshadowed the radiance of Soul, but that was all a trick of the ego. Just like the volcano it is nestled up-on, the island of the Gods rocketed up to the surface the incongruencies that still veiled my Soul so I could face them, as the weight of my own deception plummeted me down to earth.

What began as writing to express my voice in those times of fear and uncertainty became the wisdom and guidance that helped me make sense of it all. Something was writing back to me from within. All I had to do was commit to being there, no matter what state I was in, in the very early hours of the morning so it could communicate back to me.

Was it my heart? My divine channel? My Soul? To me, they are all the same, and quickly, this turned into the pathway to liberate myself yet also open to what was emerging. What had me feeling stuck and entrenched in the lasso of thinking released when I wrote. When I wrote, I was free. I sank beneath the waves of my conscious mind to land, gently, back on the soft earth of being.

During the months of despondency that preluded this writing, I had searched high and low for discourse that might have helped explain the seemingly solitary expanse of the void I was experiencing, yet my search was futile. When I felt this lost, I hunted for connection, for some piece of hope that I wasn't alone – that someone else had survived what I was going through – and had made it out the other side with their life and their sanity intact, yet radically transformed.

These words are the silent echo I heard whispering to me from the abyss. They are written in the form of letters directed to the Soul, who responds through wise compassionate direction or expanded awareness through contemplation.

These words are universal and speak to all those who have gone in search of or are still in search of something that is not easily found. Not easily found, but worth all the time, all the pain, all the hardship, and the devoted and unwavering belief that you can save yourself and find peace. For you are the only one who can.

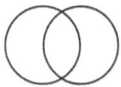

Introduction to the Love Letters

Soul is found in subtlety. Not in the intensity of the spirit realms that have been frequented by meditators and the superconscious for so long a time. Not in the visions, not in the voices, not in the feelings, but in the void. In the expansiveness of nothing.

Surrendering into space, or the void, becomes vaster and even more disconcerting, when after years of feeling ecstatic vibrations pulsing momentum and direction in life, feeling 'spirited with purpose', there becomes only the experience of nothing. Questions arise when all that has come to be known as 'home' – whether it be family, career, body, environment or sacred practice – a place designated as a sanctuary for 'self' no longer feels so. The familiarity that once upheld a sense of belonging now feels desolate and lifeless. It is no longer a space of certainty and fulfilment. The terrain is now unknown and unchartered, so drastically opposing to all that had been experienced.

THIS experience is not the one talked about. THIS is NOT what is taught. Not what one prepares for. Not what we are told. There is the belief that the journey will take us higher and higher and higher. Ascend, ascend, ascend! It does not speak of the pitfalls, the holes or the end of the road completely.

On the initial venture into the realm of self-awareness, it is easy to get swept up in a tide of grace. Being carried on a current of love and joy, floating peacefully and blissfully ignorant of life's entanglements, which have chosen to be bypassed. There may even unfold a desire to walk away from life as it is known, discarding responsibility, mundane living and endless demands in favour of the pursuit of spiritual liberation. This enamour radically reshapes and remoulds existence into a transcended state of meditation, where rose-coloured glasses become the lens of choice with which to view the world. Within this intoxicating high, the long-forgotten memory of a distant place (call it Heaven, call it God/Goddess, call it Oneness, the Universe, Om, Turiya; the state where there is no longer separation) returns, and once again there is a wish is to remain there forever.

Sooner or later though, while feeling enmeshed in spirit beyond time and space, there is a pull. A quiet, humble and patient awareness urging us to re-examine, to reconnect and reconsider. Don't we remember? We were the ones who chose to leave and elected to incarnate into form. The departure from that expansive realm was born of a hunger to deepen and expand awareness both individually and collectively. Adopting the physical world of Earth and being condensed into human form offered an opportunity to evolve into even more of who we could be. Therefore, to stay and hang out in spirit whilst moonlighting in form negated the opportunity to marry our divinity with the discomfort, confrontation and chaos of our humanity, which is the untold half of human embodiment.

For what goes up must come down.

Once this realisation can no longer be denied, the path then steadily declines into a turbulent journey that we cannot fathom. To unbecome even more deeply who we thought we were. To shed a skin that we'd wrapped our existence in.

One moment we are applying the finishing touches, having built a 'life' of solid construction and polished effort, and next, the structure is condemned as unfit for living and unsafe for existing in. In that moment, we are propelled out into a space that lies beyond the safety and security of what we had deemed as 'home'. As 'me'. For it was not 'me'. It was just a structure that can be decimated, destroyed and demolished time and time and time again.

This time we are implored to leave for good and never return, for to do so would only restrict and keep small the infiniteness of Being.

If we have the courage and the unwavering resolve to do so, the prize will be freedom. We can make our home in the wilderness of Soul and know that because we have come to find comfort in what is wild and untamed, the falseness of the world can no longer blind us. The environment will gift us all we need as we have merged with it. No more illusion of separation clouding our judgement and distracting our mind, as that package we have been born into has torn apart. We'd have ripped ourselves free from the inside out.

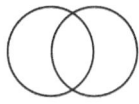

Love Letter One
Searching For You

My Beloved

For too long, I see how I have searched outside of myself to find love. To gain admiration, to feel noble despite my shortcomings, to seek adoration in the hope of securing stability and calming the uncertainty that I feel within. The love that called to me from beyond, I believed could only come from an external source.

    I have searched continuously to claim it. In validation of a job well done or through the recognition and praise of someone I love and admire. Even to the extent of searching a stranger's face for a glimmer of endorsement or through social media to garner approval. Every little transaction filled up my container of confidence and self-love that had a gaping hole in the bottom.

At times of failure, when I felt so empty, I succumbed to silencing the unworthiness I felt by placating it within the rowdiness of bars, then to finding momentary gratification through the openness of my willing legs. Yet, this didn't satisfy me for long, so when I was ready to face that truth, I changed tactic.

I searched for it in the ecstatic bliss of a drug-induced high and then felt even more vacant and alone when I descended through the floor. I sought the solitude of temples and the quiet contemplation of sacred texts and meditation. I sought You out in countries far and wide, in continents that beckoned to the brokenness I felt within. And while You left me crumbs, I still did not find You there.

I kept searching the horizon, hungrily, longingly, for any sign that You had left for me. I was prepared and ready to dive into You – You who I regarded as another human form. For I still didn't recognise my own capability as I unconsciously believed 'someone else' would save me and that if I made myself whole, pure and perfect, then You would come. Ignorantly, I was doing this purely for the benefit of self (small 's' as in selfish/egoic) as I was wanting something external for all my hard work, placing expectation and focus on what I had no control over.

So many times, I stood, eyes closed, praying that when I inhaled, You would fill me with your wandering essence and lead me closer to You. And maybe, if I parted my lips ever so slightly, You would step forward and press your tongue against mine so I could taste You. Remember You. And be intoxicated by You.

But... The wind caught my hair, yanking me backwards as I was ready to step off and into anyone's willing arms. Anyone who fulfilled that dream.

YOU, who I did not remember, but somehow KNEW, never came.

There were times I believed You had arrived. Yet, when I pulled at the fabric of reality it all began to unravel. The masquerade ended. The wolf pulled off its fleecy costume, proudly sneering in satisfaction that I had again been deceived by my own grand illusion.

BUT...

In the realms of shadow, You called me. I believed You were taunting me. Your soft and gentle voiced ached with empathetic compassion. So close were You, my lips began to tremble, my face twisting in disbelief as all the longing for You surged forth and beads of remembrance stung my eyes. You breathed life tenderly into me, and I surrendered into You as your warmth spread across my back. My shoulders softened as You drew me into You. Holding me. Supporting me. Loving me.

In love-fuelled, fervent and heartbreaking compassion, You whispered the words that I claimed as mine.

You.

Sigh.

My.

Name.

Every time I thought all was gone, all was lost, when I was left in the rubble of my own demise, Your voice was strongest. So...

WHY DID YOU NOT SHOW YOURSELF TO ME THEN!

Because you were not willing to see....
But now I do.
Now I do.
Now I see I put everything before You. Blocking You. Blocking me from You. How could You step towards me when I still held You at a distance? In that void, I filled the space with anything and everything I could find. My career, my hopes, my dreams, my infatuations and my expectations. I filled it with those who I perceived gave me the love I craved and those who most certainly did not. Vainly, I hoped, that an external object/person/situation would cover the wound that seeped longing.

It was only when You grabbed the last thing that I felt I had left, the last thing I held dear and threw it away without a care, that I could see. I could finally comprehend. I could not find the love I so desperately sought from that which was outside of me.

It was You, my Soul, my own image whose love could never be outdone by others. You were what I wanted. You were: my own love, my own validation, my own security, my own stability, my own unwavering devotion and my own unceasing faith.

That.
Was.
You.

I had been unwilling to see it until I was ready to draw my eyes to Yours. When I did, a stream of lifetimes where I had left You behind became acutely present in my mind's eye as I stepped forward into Your loving embrace. Enfolding me as I did You. Embodying me as I did You.

Opening to me as I did You. I had returned to the place I had moved away from: You.

Now. I am here. Now. You are too.

Show me how to love You, as I do not know how.

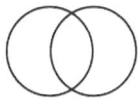

Love Letter Two
Revelations of Separation

Dear Beloved

Here I am. With You. Now. Drawn to You by a greater awareness and curiosity to want to know that which I do not. Turning within, the muffled, rhythmic beat of my own continual expansion and contraction echoes through the chamber of a body starved to be united with You. For through You is the only way I can bring my unique and individualised aspect of Spirit into form authentically. Patiently, You have been waiting for me to return home to You.
    HERE.
    NOW.
    PRESENT, in THIS moment.

To no longer be distracted by the outside world nor to be pulled into the chaos that swirls around us, fighting for our attention, our awareness. Demanding our subservience. Its hidden agenda to pull 'me' from You. From our entangled embrace, separating us. Causing us both pain and despair, though often this is not conscious. We are not aware of what has been lost, only the vague comprehension of a life we are somehow missing out on.

This is when the world 'outside' has won by claiming another hungry ego – by disconnecting it from Soul. It begins to warp what we have, what is real, what is honest and what is true. Leading me – or the preconceived idea of who I am – to believe what I want can ONLY be found outside, away from You.

This is how I was manipulated. This is how I, alone, destroyed the connection with You, my Beloved. I was lured by the flashing lights and intoxicated by sensory delights. Society swooped in and sedated me. In my small self, I was bombarded and constantly reminded that I am nothing without others. That the shadow-dancing illusion I had bought into was real, not just a play on the absence of light. That the smoke that coiled and wafted in front of the mirror was the truth. As it moved. As it lived.

But that which lies unchanging underneath, that which was obstructed from view, that which remained hidden was YOU. My Soul. My Beloved.

When I turned away from You, I saw life in small fragments of fractured light. In separation. In a single dimension. I saw, at surface level, only as much as I could see in myself. But when I turned around and looked in and not out, back to You, I saw with new eyes.

No longer was I searching a land of broken hearts and disembodied souls. I saw beyond the bright, shiny objects that glistened in the sun, drawing my attention and focus.

Blinding me.

Seducing me.

Captivating me.

The show was so beautiful. Alluring. Completely, all encompassing.

But something was missing.

It was You.

My Soul.

My lack of connection with You projected into the world around me. Search though I might, You only became more elusive.

Finally, I turned to what was behind me. The shadow I was running from. The darkness that covered my existence, my sight and perception. I turned to face You. To love all that I seemingly was not. I sat in overwhelming darkness and solitude and allowed the shadow to devour me.

No more avoidance this time.

No alcohol-induced stupors to deaden me.

No sexual encounters to engulf me.

No drug-infused highs to overcome me.

No prescribed medicine to numb me.

Just me.

Just us.

Alone. In the darkness.

Who are you? You ask.

I give you my name, and You show me I am not this.

Again, You ask:

Who are you?

I give You my job, and You show me I am also not that.

Again, You ask:

Who are you?

I give You my purpose, my attributes, my qualities, my character, my hopes and my dreams. I give You my beliefs – who I think I am. And when I think I have nothing left, You show me I am none of those.

Again, You ask:

Who are you?

I am *nobody*.

No-body.

Silence.

The infinite night enfolds me. And I am sucked down. And down. And down. Welcome to the void. Get comfortable. You might be here a while…

Then, You whisper:

All is well. I am here with you.

I always have been, even when you have not been willing to see.

We are here together.

I am showing you.

Now we can begin.

Lead on, my Beloved

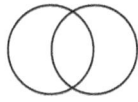

Love Letter Three
The Fall

Dear Beloved

I feel I have descended from the realm of light. From the heavens. From the stars. From the lofty ranks of a successful, accomplished life. Now I am here with all that I had forgotten. All that has been suppressed. All that has been criticised, ignored and rejected.

Not so long ago, I took flight to a place away from the discomfort of existence I was feeling. Away from monotony and routine. Away from the pressures and demands of life. Away from society's ideals, labels and expectations. I chose to disassociate rather than simply survive what I had been willing to accept as existence. I sought escape in the ecstatic bliss of an unseen world that unfolded behind closed eyes. Although it felt light and breezy, fluid, impartial, so angelic, You were not there. But I steadfastly believed You were.

In my transcendent state, I felt that I had left the land of desire behind, as it was bad, evil and sinful. I had excused myself from the immobility that bound me to my human form and resided in the lower parts of my body, my belly and my sex.

But I had just bypassed them, defiantly casting away the humanness of being.

I had taken the super freeway to an intoxicating high and altered state of mind. I had been told, I had been lectured and I believed that one had to take flight and leave this prison of body for it will only keep one in suffering. Keep one here in this mortal coil of existence, and HERE is not where one wants to be. It was somewhere else – beyond.

Up there.

Out there.

So, I pushed and fought and extracted myself as much as I could from human existence. I unbound myself. I shook off my earthly form. I became a visitor in my own body.

Who was this person who existed here?

A hermit who lived on pride.

A recluse who sought validation for efforts endured.

A cardboard individual who was drier than any religious discourse.

An individual whose righteous intellect and sense of superiority only caused further fragmentation in a world already filled with pain.

There was no life.

There was no love.
There was only a deadening pulse that cried out.
That wanted to be acknowledged.
That wanted to be embodied.
That wanted to beat wildly with…
Excitement,
Joy
and
Soul.
But I shut it all down. My mind ruled and thrived on the rigidity of discipline. On berating myself. On denying myself. On torturing myself. I was graceful and deceitful. I was euphoric and false. I fooled all those around me. Everyone believed my play.
Including me.
Including me.
I had denied so much of who I was, thrown it all back into the shadow as I ascended up and out of my being. Away from my own shortcomings. Until…
I was booted out.
Denied.
Declined.
In my meditations, the realm that existed somewhere above me was no longer open for business. The call-connect to the Divine had been cut.
I tried with all my effort to draw myself up, to rise, but I was being pulled in the opposite direction. I got slammed back to the ground and drawn into the darkness. Back into Your loving, waiting arms. Fought it all, I did, only to end up exhausted. I asked myself:

'What if I gave up the fight? What if I allowed this feeling of helplessness to consume me, overcome me and drown me?'

Then I could die while living into YOU.

At once, I could see myself sitting in a sewer. Inhaling dank, musty air. Darkness claimed me with every breath, but I was no longer afraid. No longer was I fighting to uphold an image I was not. I was no longer scared. I was stable – and I had not been stable in a very long time. Above was a latticed manhole. Light filtered in through the cracks. What was needed could come in, but I could no longer go up and out.

Now I was here.

Now I had returned.

Now it was time to begin – to see in the shadow.

To pull out all that I had thrown in. This space was too crowded and overrun with my junk. It was time to sort through, time to extricate You from where I had cast You. To find You again underneath it all.

Now I step towards You.

No longer away.

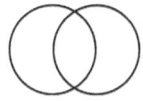

Love Letter Four
The Pledge

Dear Beloved

The one I need to love above all others. The one I now choose to cherish above all others. The one I now devote myself to, above all others. Only when I unite with You do I feel whole, do I feel that I can accomplish anything – that I am good enough.

You pull me into Your loving embrace, and I breathe a sigh of relief knowing that You have me.

Even when I do not see You.
Even when I do not hear You.
Even when I do not feel You.
You are there.

Though I doubt, as that is what the world has taught me. Doubt. Fear. Deny. Repress.

But when I turn myself back to You, when I turn around inside and go deeper in, the wings of my heart open and my chest expands. My shoulders drop away from my ears and there is a warmth that radiates from my chest, and I know You are there.

You. Are. There.

In the smallest and subtlest ways, I 'feel' Your presence. Your hand delicately touching and spontaneously manoeuvring events, people and conversations. I can 'feel' Your dusted fingerprints all over these encounters.

Nudge. Nod. Wink.

You encourage me to keep moving in a certain direction even when it makes no sense, intuition guiding me and coincidence being the signposts leading the way. These are the moments when I KNOW You are there. For how could I have gotten to that place if You had not cleared the path for me to do so?

You know I hate surprises. My dominating and controlling nature seeks to overshadow the beauty of synchronicity. But, this does not dampen Your playful nature so You continue to leave these offerings for me. You long to see the astonished and deeply appreciative look on my face when I realise what You have manifested – to remind me of Your presence, Your love and Your devotion to me.

You wait, peeping over my shoulder in anticipation as You feel the ripple of excitement surge through me, flooding my body with knowing. You revel in that feeling. It is so intoxicating and addictive for You to know that I am awash with joy, with gratitude – with awareness of You.

You want this for me for all time. But sometimes this cannot be.

Sometimes You have to take that which I love most away from me. You never want to. It pains You to have to carry out that which You know I will grow from. It makes You sad. It breaks the heart. And causes us to separate as I doubt You yet again.

But You are far stronger than I.

You know this must happen, even at the expense of me banishing You. But You still love me. You will always love me. No matter how far I stray You are always there. Sometimes You appear closer, sometimes further away. The only one who ever moves is me.

You never give up on me. In my daydreams, in my sleep, in my waking state, whenever I am open enough to hear You whisper to me, with infinite love and devotion:

Just trust.

Believe I have You.

For You know that however painful this might be, it is for my own benefit, my own wisdom, my own expansion. Rough seas will not stay that way always. You long for the calm as much as I do. For You know that is when I willingly open the gates and welcome You back into the sanctuary of my heart. When I return to Self, I am home with You.

But You cannot force those gates of my heart to open, demanding my submission and allegiance. No, you allow me to stay away as long as I choose to suffer. The threshold to my heart opens from the inside, not out. The gate cannot be pried open by external forces, no matter how much in my mind I believe they can be.

It is only when that which is outside has perished do I recall that there is a love even deeper than the one I had just lost. Even more powerful. Even more true.

It is eternal.

It is You.

I turn around and step through the open gates as I am welcomed home once more. I weep for how I castrated You. I weep for my ignorance. I weep for Your forgiveness. You pull me back into Your expansive, loving embrace. You hold me and You soothe me. You comfort me and we both know there is nothing to forgive. For this is the way it had to be. And so, it is.

And so. It is.

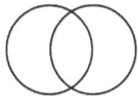

Love Letter Five
Turning Inwards

Dear Beloved

The more I turn inwards towards You, the more You reveal to me. Everything I had cast away from me that I did not want to acknowledge came to rest in the land of shadow, and You kept it safe.

Now that I am here with You, all I had turned away from in the past is awaiting my attention and my loving devotion. I did not want to have to confront these deeper aspects of myself. When I was confronted by them, I pushed them down and hid them away, or threw them behind me, believing the light in front of me was the TRUE representation of who I was.

Little did I know.

Light shines brightest against a backdrop of shadow.

All that I had nonchalantly disregarded had pooled into a heaped mess, slowing my progress. Unknowingly, I hauled it around. Cumbersome, awkward and oppressive. I would not bring my attention to it as the lure of the light beckoned me. No one spoke of turning around, of confronting what pulled me down and drew me back or of the comfort and solace I would find when I returned to You.

I was too high – ego-driven – believing I had transcended the heavy matter of my existence. I believed that what was in the darkness, in shadow, was not important.

You called to me, but I did not listen.

I did not want to hear.

I did not want to know.

Best to stay in the light.

Be happy.

Be grateful.

Be false and one dimensional.

I did not want to admit my shortcomings – that I was not being authentic – for then I could remain within the realms of respectability and social acceptance. Because, who willingly ventures to hell to confront their demons? Disinclined to do so, I lived on the surface, though I believed I had penetrated far deeper layers. I drank tea and spoke of pleasantries while serving cake and ignoring the creatures climbing the walls and tearing the curtains to get my attention.

One more pill should do it. That will pacify these hungry beasts vying to be acknowledged.

The more I refused to turn and face You and all that I had denied, the more it haunted me. Your slender fingers clutched at my shoulders, gently pulling me back. Wistfully reminding me of that which lay in the darkness. I was scared of You, of Your power, as I knew it would undo my perfectly cultivated image. The light I falsely shone which I believed was my radiance, my character and true expression, was burning a hole through this illusion as I could no longer be masked by the lie.

I was stalked by those fearsome creatures that guarded my vault of secrets and prowled the recesses of my mind. Little did I realise that they were my own creations, my projections I was afraid of, which had manifested as threatening forms. I was unwilling to turn towards them in the darkness and face the fear that was dictating the narrative of my life.

When walking the path of light, all is illuminated.

All is seen.

All is known.

All is clear.

This is not the gift of darkness. In darkness I could not find my way. I could not see the path. I could not feel the path. I was no longer even certain there was a path. There was just, seemingly, nothing. Initially. Not the story nor creatures I had created, nor the drowning of intense emotions, just a listless boat on an ocean of melancholy. There was simply nothing – when there had always been something.

And in nothing did I find that I too was nobody.

I was not the image I portrayed:

the accreditations,

the certifications,

the awards,

the praise,

or the shame.

Nothing.

In allowing the nothing to unfold, I became no-body, I was set free. When there is nothing, there is nothing to lose. Beneath it all, sitting back and smiling, joyously, was You.

Unchanging.

As You had always been.

As You will always be.

Eternal.

There are no discrepancies in a person's soul. Only ignorance and flaws of character when there is a blockage within the engorging ego.

When I turned and faced You, I saw who I was.

Love.

Pure love.

Not something that had to be cultivated. Not something that needed to be worked on. I was simply THAT.

I AM THAT.

I AM THAT.

The surface may alter. The waves of chaos and tribulation may crash upon the shore of my being, but at the bottom of the ocean You sit and wait. Reminding me…

I AM THAT.

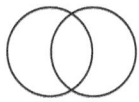

Love Letter Six
Sacred Union

Dear Beloved

I love all the small and intricate ways You remind me that You are here.

When You take my hand and flow Your words through the cursive of my pen. When Your words are breathed out through my mouth, even I am floored at the wisdom I hear. When You raise the heat in my body and my heart swells with recognition, I can 'feel' I have merged with You – that we are one, that there is no distance between You and I.

You leave small reminders for me throughout the day to show me You are thinking of me – that You are right there with me. That cup of coffee, brought to me by a friend. The fragrance that emanates from flowers at sunrise, bursting with Your essence. The serendipitous meeting in a cafe and a shared conversation. Or the meeting of eyes across a room with someone who has found the same thing. They too have found You, and we recognise that in each other. Those moments are bliss. Those moments hold a lifetime in a single gaze.

You shake the world around me. It trembles with arduous passion as it longs for me to reach out and touch it. Touch You. As You are, as I am. I can love every bee, every bird, every flower, every sunset. Because in every moment, You call out to draw me back into this 'present' fold – to remind me of Your beauty and my own beauty, reflected in the environment (as we are one, in nature).

You say to me:
I play in daylight hours
and dance on moonlit nights.
I move all those in contact with me,
even when
I am not seen.
I am one with all
and all is one with me,
for you will see
we are the same.
Not a separate entity.
I live as a tree's solid form.
I live as the bird in the sky.
I am the sun.
I am the air.
I am the life you breathe.
Soul does not end with you,
it extends to all life forms.

When you reach in to touch me,
you touch the world at its core.

In the stillness is when You expand. Your presence fills the gap in-between the beginning and endings of thought. You are the pause. A break in the continuum. A moment of clarity punctuating a symphony of needs, demands, mind chatter and background noise. Your subtle grace is the gift slicing through it all. The world is saturated with Your love, with Your devotion, but for too long I have just been too blind to see it.

The quieter I become, the more I can hear You. Your voice amplifies when space is created and I can entice You to come share Your loving wisdom with me. Within this union, my own energy and frequency is turned up as there is no longer simply 'me', but us. Together. Building a bridge between worlds and closing the gap so the formless can take form. Yet, my mind struggles to make sense of this. It is not logical or coherent but I am being implored to put my doubts aside and trust in what is not seen, only felt.

You show me You are here, and I put it down to fate or luck. I am reluctant to acknowledge Your presence. You who is manifesting from within me, creating the world I perceive. When I see through Your eyes everything is so perfect and connected. The landscape shifts from hostile and isolated to abundant and intricately woven. Only in detaching from You do I feel separate. Insignificant. Small. You show me more than I can 'see'. I cannot comprehend your devotion – your continued patience humbles me.

I now know that all You seek is acknowledgement – a smile, a thank you for showing me that this was You. That

You seek to show me every day, in every moment how much I am loved, how much I am adored and how worthy I am. That You love ME above all else. That what You want is the very thing that I want. You will stop at nothing to help me achieve it. Because that is how much You love me.

    That is how much
    You
    Love
    Me.

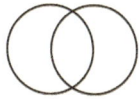

Love Letter Seven
It Will Not Be the Last

Dear Beloved

When I surrender, You pick me up and carry me forward. Only when I wave the white flag and lay down my arms, calling a ceasefire to my battle with You, can You step forward. You soothe me and nurture me in my exhaustion following the torturous fights I endure day and night. Day in. Day out.

    I have sent messages of control, willpower and determination out in every direction, wanting to determine every aspect of my life. I placed a crown reverently upon the authority of reason, which ruled from the lofty throne of practicality. I believed that through force I could make everything bend to my will and manipulate the unseen world in accordance with what I deemed best.

But my own sense of power was insignificant and pitiful when I believed I could control You. Defy You I tried, though I never succeeded. I was only left battered and bruised by my attempts.

Still, I would not give up. I knew what I wanted. I knew which way I wanted to go, and all I wanted for You to do was simply follow along.

BUT...

Your vision saw far beyond what I could. You resisted and withheld me from edging too far down a path I believed was the 'way', for You knew that would lead me further into illusion.

You chuckled with heartfelt compassion at the stern and forceful way I tried to lead You down MY path. I gave no consideration to You, to OUR path. I made life so difficult; everything was such a struggle. Despite the seemingly obvious indicators to stop, I ploughed forward in the wrong direction... though never got far.

Your laugh was always so joyous when I attempted those plots. I could hear the muffled giggle rolling from deep within me, tempting my sterner self. You were not laughing at me but coaxing me to join You and fall to the ground in hysterics. Because this joke was hilarious. The only one who did not find it funny was me.

Where did joy go in those days? As this was what I had banished. Along with fun. Along with spontaneity. Along with You. You and the company You kept were a threat to all that I wanted and sought to acquire, for nothing could be easily obtained without effort, right? I staunchly believed that to get anywhere in life, it had to be with focused, determined effort. There was no time to play.

Life is serious.

Don't You know?

No. You do not know. Because that has never been your way. Your way has always been 'love'.

To come back to You I had to traverse mountains of agony, rivers of pain, oceans of sadness and endure the crippling reality of aloneness. The reason I had to was because I was the one who had created all that distance, all that space, and built a whole world in that void. The void between You and me.

When I could take no more and I willingly chose to return, it was the longest journey to endure – to find the way home to You, my Soul.

But now I am here with You. You are leading me and showing me the way. How abundant, beautiful and unexpected my life has become since I have allowed You to guide me. To lead me to places, situations and adventures I would not have been able to experience without Your guiding hand.

You take me where I am scared to go but You take me and show me You are with me. Beside me, behind me and within me, cheering me on to take the next step. Because even this next step will not be my last.

This next step will not be my last…

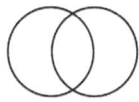

Love Letter Eight
Poised and Ready

Dear Beloved

Shadow looms ominously before me, commanding both attention and respect. For this is where I left You, entangled in all the pain of the past I'd adamantly pushed away as it was too confronting to face. Having avoided it time after time, I lost more and more of my Self, and You, who was entwined in it all. I became nothing more than a human doing because the being, which was You, was scarcely able to penetrate the walls I had built to keep out the torrent of emotion from drowning me.

    I now stand poised and ready, willing to face what I haven't before. Ready to turn around and glance behind me. Ready to look over my shoulder and into the void in the hope of seeing You there. Having finally remembered that you extend back into all that has come to pass. In all that has already been. You've been behind me every step of the way, protecting my back. Now You invite me to about-face and walk towards You and reclaim all that I have suppressed.

Images gather in my mind.

Memories unfold their wings, taking flight across the landscape over a chaotic ocean of confusion.

And I remember.

When I had begged 'why?' in agony
and all I got was silence.
That person,
that situation,
that loss,
that pain
or that heartbreak,
was meant to return to me now.
Return to me
so that I can understand,
so I can 'see'.

Your guiding hand had moved me in a direction that I did not understand, in a way I could not comprehend, trapped by the limited capacity of sense.

You held the remembrance of it
in the cave of shadow,
when I had banished it to the land of the forgotten.
You held it tightly
to return it to my expanded consciousness.
When I was ready.

As the fullness of experience takes shape, everything fits together – textures, grooves and contours aligning. My missing pieces have found a home.

My missing pieces have found a home.

Only now can I truly behold the exquisite execution of their placement, as radically distorted I once believed those moments to be. Yet You, my Beloved, knew I would be awed and would honour their placement in due time, as I do now.

You are the one at my back, protecting the forgotten and collecting all I discard, believing it is not important. Dutifully picking up the experiences I label as 'bad' when I throw them away. For in that rubbish lies jewels of wisdom, but I cannot see that yet.

You merely chuckle and clutch them to you, as a parent does with neglected toys that once brought joy. Returning them to the box of memories as You know the forgotten remnants will be cried for at another time. They bring comfort and soothe the temper, the tantrum and defiant resistance to accept all that is. That is when the 'why' becomes the 'known'. The forgotten becomes illuminated and the insignificant becomes important.

They are the memories that shift perspectives and alter consciousness. YOU know the impact would be great, which is why I had to experience it in the past to gain its knowledge in the present. Nothing happens sequentially. Plot twists always keep me guessing, amused and constantly laughing at the divine play You direct me in.

It is all just one play. Many characters. One story.

Do not take it all so seriously.
The conclusion is the same for all.

Alana Grainger

So be in the present.
Have fun.
And live.
Live as if tomorrow it is all going to come to an end.
For it is unknown when it will.

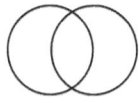

Love Letter Nine
The Power of 'Yes'

Dear Beloved

When I say 'yes' You step forward. When I allow myself to trust in all that is unseen and unknown, then You reveal to me abundance, beauty and magic.

'Yes' is the current that flows in the law of attraction, that purrs in the essence of Soul. Though, this can only be fulfilled when I have acknowledged and upheld the sacred 'no'. 'No' to what doesn't serve me; 'no' to what makes me feel small; 'no' to self-sacrificing for others; 'no' is the boundary upholding it all. 'No' to time wasting and distractions; 'no' to overthinking and perfection; 'no' to endlessly doubting myself; 'no' is the current of reconnection. 'No', to anything on the outside that doesn't align with the expansive inner 'yes'. For the two are interlinked. The sacred yes and no are both threads in the knit of devotion, fashioned from the tapestry of love. These words are channels through which the path of love is either being honoured or denied. The submissive, (small) self-centred yes and no, are simply their sacred opposites that do not have the courage to be spoken.

'Yes' in its fullness, picks me up and continues to carry me effortlessly downstream to offerings that could not have been reached if I had held myself back with a shallow, ego-driven 'no' so as to play safe.

When I harness myself to this current, my body tingles with excitement and potential, wanting to embrace life in all its fullness. I feel the reverberations of my heart pounding possibilities through my veins and urging me to take action as I become both hot and cold, fearful and thrilled. The curious part of me is eager to step forward and go beyond the safety net of submissiveness. If I can do this then, the quantum realm will take note of the profound yet subtle change and will realign to meet this greater resonance and new consciousness. The silent symphony of energy echoing through the natural world orchestrates continual expansion and ever unfolding growth that I can merge with. All I have to do is choose yes and step forward into what is unknown as I want to be alive and not merely existing.

To say yes is to surrender the ego.

To say yes is to trust.

To say yes is to relinquish control – of life and of love and of what feels safe and known.

To say yes is to free myself of a future I had planned in my mind that was not real, that was just a projection I thought would serve me.

And be guided to something that will benefit me more.

Even if it doesn't make sense.

'Yes' can take me to places I have yet to imagine – on adventures of the Soul and explorations of untapped potential. To say yes is to let life in.

When I say no from my mind, I believe I know better. I become arrogant and defiant. Having already envisioned a future in which I am successful, powerful and affluent for this means I've made it? No? Oh, I don't need Your opinion or approval. The way is forward, beckons the ego. There has to be a plan. Steps. Guidelines. Boundaries. Strategies executed. That is how to build a house from the ground up. But life is not a house, though sometimes it would be easier to apply those principles to plot the general trajectory.

Life is more like nature. No set rules, just permission to grow.

We are of that world.

We are from that world.

When we return to that world we remember

that life is easier when it is not pushed

but invited to unfold from within.

Saying no from a place of logic stops us dancing along the path of life. 'No' means a halt to joyously skipping through the day, as the forgotten memory of now no longer exists. 'No' has relegated the mind to be in the future. Or the past. 'No' is the slave driver whipping my sorry arse to work harder.

'Dreams come at a price!' says the voice of 'no'.

'There is no fun on the path to success.'

'You cannot get to that point you want by playing, singing and laughing,' my mind cruelly taunts.

'No' craves rigidity, for that is all it knows. But I can be defiant and cause a system overload when I say yes from my heart. I can melt the barriers I have built. I can rewire my circuit board. I can go against all that I have been programmed to implement. 'Yes' is the current of freedom, when it is spoken from the heart, the way to fluidly get me to my purpose.

For 'yes' is sacred when pledged from a place of love and spoken aloud into the realm of the unknown. It opens a doorway and begins to build a bridge between what is known and that which is not.

'Yes' belongs to the realms of the divine.

'Yes' belongs to spirit

and to Soul.

'No' from the thinking mind belongs to society and the preconceived ideas of who we think we should be.

'Yes' has taken me to now. For where I am now was once a dream that 'yes' led me to. To get to where I want to be, I just have to keep following my sacred 'yes', when all I want to say is no and close down, hide and protect myself.

'Yes' is expansive and continues to pry me open.

'Yes' is growth.

'Yes' is the precursor to evolve.

'Yes' brings me back to You.

So, today I am going to follow You.

For You will lead me when I simply say yes.

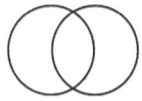

Love Letter Ten
The Ring Master

Dear Beloved

Vulnerability is Your ring, where I, the carnivorous beast, fight to defend my softest parts.

You crack the whip, and I roar in defence and defiance – not wanting to succumb to defeat. I fight and swipe at You, but You pirouette, spinning gracefully away from my violent eruptions, elegantly regaining Your position. Poised and commanding, You flash a loving and adoring smile in my direction. It does little to soften my wild and relentless fight against You. I prowl and skulk and turn my mouth up in obvious disdain, staring You down.

You ask me to yield, and I fight You at every turn. You have me beguiled, though. I could flee the ring but if I stay and confront You, I believe I will eventually win. The realm of vulnerability will once again be mine, and You will be powerless to tame me. I believe I can launch myself upon You and tear You limb from limb. But You are always one step in front, knowing my moves before I do.

You persist as You know I want this – not to be tamed but to be free.

On the surface I fight it, but deep down You know this is what I want. Underneath, vulnerability is all I desire. Fear is the cloak that hides it. When standing in that ring of vulnerability I want to protect all that I have become as I fear the next step will somehow undo it all. The more I rear up, the closer I experience your stern, fervent love. For freedom can only be reached while transiting the landscape of vulnerability. There is no way around it but through it.

A soft growl escapes my lips.
I lower my body in submission.
Belly on sawdust, paws on the ground.
My eyes lock on to your formidable form.
You hold my gaze and step forward.
Hand lowered, whip dropped.
You step towards me, and I do not flinch.
You take another step, and I lower my head.
I am done with fighting.
I am done with war.
I would rather be YOUR Beloved
than your beast.

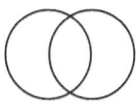

Love Letter Eleven
Baptism of Truth

Dear Beloved

I can see that the only one who withheld me from love, is me.

I blamed You and scorned You. Thrusting all of my unjust feelings of denial upon You. YOU were the one withholding everything from me, placing all that I wanted beyond reach. I mistakenly believed You were playing a sick little game and I was no more than a marionette that danced for Your entertainment.

I was simply not willing to look at my own reasons for sabotage. It was easier to blame an external form of my unconscious self than it was to bring light to the darkest places. It was easier to say:

'This happened "to" me.'

Not: 'I made this happen.'

When I took responsibility, the only one who was left to change the circumstances was me. Only I could heal my pain. I loved the struggle as much as I did the suffering it inflicted. I was some kind of masochist, but it is the existence of the wounds that allows awakening to happen. In the bitter agony of my discomfort, when I began to unravel the seams of my frayed being, was where You lay.

The closer I got to darkness, the more I submerged myself in it and the less frightened I became. Only in the chasm of suffering could the healing begin. In reclaiming the experience that I felt broken by could I tentatively set about watering the barren soil with forgiveness. Forgiveness towards myself for being in that situation, towards all those involved as I was done with blame. Forgiveness for the time lost and for the pain I'd caused others because of my own unhealed wounds. I turned over the fragile ground, split and segmented by rivers of self-loathing that separated each piece from the other. A flood of remorse surged forth, hungrily soaked up by this desert soulscape, and then You, my Beloved, could receive me as I had returned to You at last. As the waters encircled us, Your enduring presence – moved by my devotion – engulfed me with truth. Insights drenched my awareness with profound wisdom.

I swam in the deepest waters of Soul.
I bathed in all that I had forgotten to be.
I was cleansed with a sense of my own pain
and felt it washing over me.
So cathartic and grounding was my longing
to return to this place and be free

to uncover what lay beneath my scars
and no longer feel the urge to flee.
Here is where You enveloped me,
drew me close and pulled me down,
and this time I did not fight you.
I simply let myself drown.
In all that I was,
in all that I had been,
in all that I now am.
And I knew
I would not die,
because You,
My Beloved,
had
Me.

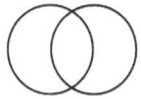

Love Letter Twelve
Divine Timing

Dear Beloved

Oh, what miraculous offerings You place before me when I open my eyes to see!

Now, more than ever, as I am coming to know You, have I come to comprehend the divine timing in everything. Nothing will happen a moment too soon or too late. You expertly guide me to places where I meet people unexpectedly and form connections that turn into unfathomable opportunities. If I hadn't left precisely when You had nudged me to leave, to reluctantly follow my friends 'out', to accept the offer to go on a weekend away, to move to a place I knew very little about…I wouldn't be where I find myself now.

You pull the strings that guide me along.

Beckoning me with your silent echo.
I believe the path I walk is my own.
As I know the right direction.
As I know the correct trajectory.
As I am simply the one who knows best.
But I am in fact an instrument, a tool, a vessel
Through which The Divine, as You, can flow.
Waves of consciousness swell into, through and out of me
Until 'I' prevent its course.

When I turn and face You and recite my words of love and devotion to You, I am reminded that where I am now was once nothing more than a vision I had that lay in what was the 'future', for it was not present. From somewhere in the distance You called out to encourage me closer to You. When I got here, I did not give myself the time to acknowledge the climb, or appreciate the view. I did not take time to catch my breath or even acknowledge You. I just wanted to keep climbing and see what lay at the top of the next plateau.

Rest for a while.
Take a moment to see where you are,
how far you've come
and the collection of experiences shouldered.
Whilst the path you walk may still be long
your capacity to stride forward
hinges on integrating your past
and resolving all that lies in shadow.
Nudge, nod, wink.
GRIN.

A dream I once had is now my reality, is now my everyday existence.

In my days of arrogance and self-involvement, I believed I got here all by myself, but the reality is starkly different. If I had not begun to turn to You and hear You whispering Your words of encouragement and belief in the coma of my subconscious, I would still be 'waiting' for life to happen. I had to be the first one to take a step towards You, to call out and ask for Your assistance. You were always willing and always ready, but I had been too proud to ask.

When I took a step towards You,
You took two towards me.
You had longed for me
to return.
I'd now begun
the journey
that will take me
my entire life
to comprehend.

Everything happens precisely when it is meant to. No amount of pushing can hasten the process.

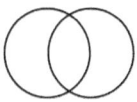

Love Letter Thirteen
The Silent Echo

Dear Beloved

Why is it that awakening is more often seen through a linear lens? This is a limited and dogmatic way to view the expansiveness of what is 'becoming'. Ascension and descending then simply become two points on a highway to ride along. One state leading inextricably to the other, yet not taking into account the frequent detours and messy navigation that comes with this journey.

You have shown me a different way. A more integrated way. One that unfolds. The petals of wisdom innate to my own process of transformation unfurl under the warmth and receptivity of surrender into You. It is as if I am falling off a chair, back into a larger part that is undeniably me. When I finally submit to embracing the void, I find stillness. I amplify in this stillness, and in beingness, I awaken to the possibilities, insights and truth. From a place of grounded authenticity, conscious action blooms.

To the untrained eye, it may only look like we are growing up, but we expand into every direction, our capacity to stand resolute in sacred space increasing. As a flower continues to peel back its beauty in graceful, elegant movements, so too do we continue to open outwards exposing our heart to the world.

But this awareness is not something that can be broken through, ripped open or forcibly pushed. It is much softer and subtler than that. You come in when I soften, not when I harden. You cannot approach me when I am so caught up in my head and body of 'doing'. Only when I feel 'broken', bereft with the collapse of what I had known can You enter in through the cracks and steer me towards what is honest, what is true.

You return to me in cycles. When I block You out and silence You, then You retreat back into the depths and wait for an opportune time when I am ready to listen. When I am lost, when I feel alone, when the outside world can no longer offer me the very thing I want, You can. In those times You again step forward and embrace me. In those times too do I remember and recall You. Now, though, I am dedicated to You. I am enamoured by You. You have bewitched me and mystified my being so the only thing I want is connection to You. As I step forward, I have found:

The closer I get to You, the subtler You become.

A game of hide and seek ensues.

No longer do You have to scream,

yell
or shout
to get my attention.
You know I am waiting
for the hint of a whisper
to escape Your lips.
In longing,
in anticipation,
I edge myself ever closer
to You
and wait for Your words
to echo silently
back to me.

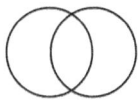

Love Letter Fourteen
Confronting Vulnerability

Dear Beloved

There are times when I feel so scared, so raw and confronted by all that is surrounding me, the atmosphere dense and charged with the current of growth. I lack the ability of perspective and cannot see beyond the moment that is holding me prisoner, taunting me with defeat.

While I am reluctant to step forward, You equally do not let me shrink back, as You know that I am more than this. More than the desire of wanting to return to what I know, what is familiar, as that does not serve me. It only serves to keep me small. You know I want more than that.

Now that I have come to meet You and I know You are my staunch drill sergeant, my benevolent mother, my celebratory cheer leader and my passionate lover, You refuse to let me return to my previous form. You will not stand and allow me to cower, backing into my shrunken lower self that feels unable to take a stand for all I believe in and for what I hold true.

The closer I get to my dreams, the larger and more unrealistic they tower in front of me. No longer are they distant mountains whose peaks I envision scaling. They are now a jagged rocky incline rising steeply before me. No plateau in sight, no place to stop and breathe, just a wall of solid rock before me.

Climb. You urge softly, sweetly, tenderly.

Just trust. Believe I have you.

But I do not.

I stay rooted to the spot.

Climb. You say, a little more encouragingly.

Strong warm hands on my shoulders

edging me to step forward.

But I do not.

Climb. You say, with authority and firmness.

But I do not.

I am not moving.

I have made my decision.

But You know better.

So you show me my life where I have succumbed to allowing the opinions of others to cripple me and hold me back. The anxiety of being devoured by some monster my mind has created or something I deem the world will launch upon me, pales in comparison to the anguished lament of having not tried at all. Wasted, withered, tired and forlorn, I sense I become nothing but a desolate landscape stripped of life force as I had denied my own life force.

This propels me forwards and upwards, taking action to do this purely for me. Better to fall whilst climbing than get eaten alive by fear.

You always give me ample opportunities to jump before I am pushed. You can see I don't want to move into that place of vulnerability as it is 'unknown' and I cannot have control in the unknown.

There is no rudder to guide the course of my life in the unknown. But for me to enter into the next realm, this part of the journey calls for vulnerability, which dissolves the ego. It calls me to seek humility in the face of an unpredictable outcome. To move into and explore the space that I have been ignorant of or flat out denied, and mine the shafts for the elusive gold within. When found, a beacon of truth, a shard of remembrance, a prism of light becomes illuminated as the doorway to divinity has opened and You, my Beloved, step forward regally into me. Only in reclaiming the darkness does inspirational power dwell, the power that lights the lamp within.

If I can drop my character, my personality and my ego (which is the quilt that I have wrapped You up in for protection), if I can let You shine through, if I can throw off these covers, exposing the unique essence of that which I AM and which is begging to be expressed, then life will realign to meet this new frequency. Everything wanted lies on the other side of fear, and boldly I now choose to let You take centre stage.

The projection of rejection is far worse than its actual experience. Residual pain can only be felt in a bruised ego, a flawed character or a cracked personality. When the outside does not match the inside. This is when You begin to emerge, as I have surrendered. As I am vulnerable. And here is where You can again grow larger, so as to guide me to the next place of discomfort where You can claim even more of me.

Out of protection, I placed my heart in a tower to keep it safe, but separated. I have not felt pain, nor have I felt love. I kept You out as You asked for ALL of me and I was not willing to give myself to love.

The more I begged and pleaded for someone from the outside to come and scale the tower and rescue me from myself, fewer did. Some white knights, with their own holes and Souls to fill, did approach. My cries for assistance had been heard, yet, when they gallantly stepped forward, I catapulted stones and rocks at them, calling them in but barricading myself away.

No-one could climb that wall but me. In allegiance to You, I now offer my hand thereby uniting us to claim the space of the heart as our abode. This unlocks the door to love so we can step out of the castle and onto the draw bridge. Surrendering to the deep unknown and letting the cavalry of life charge towards us. As I know that with You, I have the capacity to embrace it all.

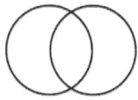

Love Letter Fifteen
Follow the Energy

Dear Beloved

With energy You drive me in the direction I need to be heading. Even when I cannot envision how I am going to get there, how I am going to maintain myself there, there is something about it that simply feels 'right'. There is something in me that knows that my future self is already living in this sphere of existence and is calling to me to step towards it.

But...

There are times when I get to the place that You have called me, and I cannot see beyond the present. It is dark, it is confined, it is limited, it is blocked. The container of my existence cannot keep going forward as the road has abruptly come to an end. So why did You call me here at all? It is only then that I can see I need to either turn left or right. Or maybe even go deeper inside to create the space that only you can fill. Certain detours are inevitable on this journey of life and liberation. The path is not one that follows a straight line, but circles – it weaves and moves in all directions.

Sometimes when I turn left or I turn right, I encounter the expansiveness I had believed lay in front of me, but was in fact, off to the side. A whole valley of opportunities and possibilities become available to me when I am able to stop smacking my head against the wall that is in front of me and simply turn in a different direction.

A different direction is not back.

A different direction changes perspective.

A different direction alters course –

often, for the better.

Sometimes, that was the only way to get where I needed to go. I had been drawn to the path that lay before me without seeing the fork in the road that lay beyond. A straight line does not always procure the way to destiny, to fulfil the reason for being here and to grant understanding and wisdom. Twists and turns are what enrich the narrative of life. The sweetness blended with the saltiness of tears; the crunch of hardships and the tang of joy. The sharpness of pain and richness of expansion add texture to the exquisiteness of human experience.

The bold,
the bland,
the tasty,
the bitter,
the sensual,

the disgusting,
the nectar,
the poison,
the contrast,
the similarity,
the sadness,
the joy –
all ingredients
to life.
If one part is missing,
one step skipped,
the final product
will be unable to rise
and will remain a heap
of under-baked potential.

So, guide me into the realm of the unknown, of all I cannot comprehend. Of all I cannot see. And redirect me when I find myself facing a wall and believing that *this* is all there is.

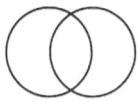

Love Letter Sixteen
In Devotion to You

Dear Beloved

How can I possibly begin to express my gratitude to You? Words feel inadequate as they simply cannot convey the gratitude and peace I now feel having You in my life. I no longer feel 'alone' as I know You are always here with me. I cannot even begin to convey the depth of my adoration and devotion – the joy of knowing You entrusted ME as your human vehicle.

Can you feel how much I love You? For when I feel whole, complete and expansive, it is because I know I have merged with You. Internally, I sense the alignment of form and formless through union in the heart as this energy beams the inner radiance into outer form. I love You even more as I know You ask little of me, aside from to trust

You and love You. For it is only through love can WE ever move into action.

I can do much, I can do little, I can be 'good', I can be 'bad' and still You will not desert me. You will love me all the same. We can embrace as one, if I have allowed You to get that close, or from a distance if I have pushed You away. But still You remain, still Your devotion to me knows no limits for we are one and the same, even when I, in my limited vision cannot see it.

If I find I can love You with complete openness and with no expectation of what You can give me, then I find You give me everything. You give me freedom when I flee, and You wait patiently for me to return. I yell and scream at You for situations that are not in my favour. I deny You; I repress You and disobey You. And still You love me. Even more so when You see I have grown because I took a stand against You. You know I will always return, that I will always come home to You.

And when we are in quiet union, when I see nothing in front of me and nothing behind me, I am peaceful and present in the unknowingness. You bring me everything I need. All I have to do is take my hooks out of the future and remove them from the past and reel all that outgoing energy back in. To just be. For beingness is the portal that allows life to move with ease and grace through me.

When I am no longer searching, no longer grappling, no longer grasping, what I desire then also begins to desire me. When I turn my attention to focus upon it and consciously let it go, the frequency of external interest is sparked. What I had been forcibly chasing down no longer feels threatened, restricted or cornered – all because my focus had returned to You, my Beloved. By doing so, what is 'outside' of me now feels free. In freedom there is ease upon which potential and expansion soar – not when I clip the wings through fear and hold it in a cage wanting it to never leave me. Then freedom dies into resentment.

Only with flight can a bird land.
If it only knew the branches of trees,
wings would hold no use.

You urge me to see the bird and watch its flight. Let the homing pigeon of dreams traverse the sky in search of what it needs. How can dreams fall into place when I grasp at tail feathers?

Your guidance enlightens me to be open to the possibilities. For when I focus too intently on a single direction then I miss the many roads I could travel along. For it is the journey, not the destination, that is important. There is not a set route. There is much earth on which to place my feet. Rocky and grassy, steep and sandy, overgrown and cleared. You lead the way, not me, not I. Despite me sometimes believing I know the path better than You. But I do not.

I love You
simply because
to not do so
creates a void
that nothing else can fill.

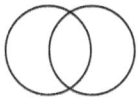

Love Letter Seventeen
The Unbecoming

Dear Beloved

I think I finally understand what You have been wanting me to see.

Hindsight can only be gained when there is substantial distance between what has passed and myself. While still tangled in the web of experience, comprehension is more often futile. All vast landscapes are better viewed from the vantage point of perspective as it is somewhat higher or 'beyond'. When in the middle of an unfolding, it is hard to see that I am anywhere else but in it. Only when the sun graces my face again can I understand that the darkness that overlaid me was indeed fertile soil stimulating growth.

When I lay lost in the darkness, uncertain of light ever returning to illuminate my path, I felt hopeless. I gave up. I simply resisted fighting my way to the top and got comfortable in all that was difficult and distressing. When I did, something began to happen. The longer I stayed and more inquisitive I became in this seemingly dense and constricting undergrowth, the stronger my intuition grew at navigating my way up to the surface. I began to 'see' but not from my eyes. There was a knowing inside unfurling, guiding me as I was finally listening. That was You.

Only now can I see what You were offering to me in the darkness, when it appeared there was no hope. When all I wanted to do was foolishly deny my reality and return to the realms of light, of buoyancy, of joy. Instead, I elected to settle into You and face what I hadn't wanted to see. No longer did I choose to search outside to help me alleviate my suffering. No longer did I seek to vacate this body and attach myself to a future that wasn't present now . You kept me here so I could learn that if I stayed with the discomfort and stayed embodied, everything I needed would somehow be guided to me. You taught me that in stillness, when I focus inwards, my frequency grows. You gave me the opportunity to allow everything to come in rather than me go out to chase it. For when I did, I detached. I severed my connection with You, my Soul.

But...

I understand now that it is not about choosing the modern world over the spiritual one or vice versa but joining and uniting the two together. You, my Soul, flow through the heart, which is the bridge where we meet and the channel that consciousness moves into, through and out of my body. I feel You getting bigger, stronger and more powerful when I stay in my body and in my heart with You.

It is not about reaching up to heaven
and drawing heaven down to earth.
But knowing that this connection exists within.
It is reached through You.
In opening to You
Heaven can live on Earth.

Then from small and silent do You grow expansive and expressive. The more attention and focus I give You, the more space You take up in me. You reclaim the land of my false and disjointed self – a hazy illusion disguised as the real me.

The illumination that radiates from me is You, breaking through all my layers of conditioning and carefully constructed character. You lovingly unwind the deceptions I'd wrapped myself tightly in and seek to clear out my ignorance as You cannot be bound by the projections of who I thought I should be. You want to claim ALL of me back, as without You, I am a vacant unit trawling through life with no meaning and no purpose.

The more You claim me
the faster and quicker
I willingly surrender
the illusions of limitation
that have been the framework
I've built my life upon.

I long to be overhauled. This renovation, overdue. Change and shift occurs, moving from the inside to out. I am done acting in life. Sitting pretty in a row alongside perfectly manicured gardens on an uninspiring residential strip, housing people who simply exist. The keys are Yours, my Beloved, remake me in Your image and remind me of who I am.

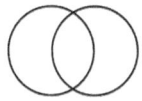

Love Letter Eighteen
Honouring Cycles

Dear Beloved

By honouring the flow and the cycles, I am becoming even more aware of them. I am bearing witness to the cycles that unfold not just monthly with the waxing and waning of the moon, but with the cycles that unfold during the day.

When the moon is full in the sky and the sun at its zenith I too am at the maximum capacity of energy and productivity. The incline up to this point has been dappled with drive, focus and expansion. When teetering at the pinnacle I can already begin to feel the downward pull. My emotions and energy begin to dive. I can try to keep them up, but I only end up fighting the natural gravitational pull. I cannot stop it.

I am learning that this is the time to take stock and review. To not begin new tasks but to skilfully apply myself to what has started and focus my attention on its completion. This nonlinear and flexible approach is free of rigidity and allows for an even greater unfolding of creativity.

In flowing with the natural rhythms and undulations of energy, life begins to glide effortlessly rather than me forcefully exerting and exhausting myself in the process. At times, resistance is encountered, though all I need do is turn within and ask You if summoning my energy to move forward is beneficial or not. For I am beginning to comprehend that what I once labelled as lazy was intuition guiding me to soften and rest, but often I pushed on despite my body telling me otherwise. This led to noticeable discomfort and dis-ease.

This precious vessel that I have been blessed with carries far more wisdom and receptivity than I give it credit for or acknowledge. It is always trying to feed messages to me that I often do not listen to or do not want to hear. There is always the pressure to do more, to be more, not simply witness and allow.

The confrontation of surrender, the relinquishing of control to something that is internal and not external is confusing. My mind tells me one thing and my body says another.

Mind: you HAVE to do this! This is important! Move! Come on! TRY HARDER!

Body: I am so exhausted. I cannot keep running at this pace. Please listen to me.

Mind: What the body is telling you is that you are not able to carry out this task. C'mon! Hustle up!

If I continue to ignore the inkling of burnout tugging at my awareness trying to inform me to redirect my energy into sustaining my inner fire, then without fail my body will soon bring it to my attention.

Body: Okay, well there were signs to course correct, and in disregarding them I am going to take you down.

I am learning to converse with my body, as my mind has ruled and driven me into the ground for far too long. My body is much more nurturing and will guide me as it is more receptive to the natural flow of life.

Having a human body ties me to nature, which is governed by the cycles of the sun and moon. In remembering that I am not a detached aspect of the environment but one and part of it, invites me to 'lean in' to this unseen movement and dance *with* the pulsation of life, not to be out of beat to it.

I can learn to rise and rest as my body deems fit and not allow the tyrannical rigidity of my mind to unnecessarily direct the way. And somewhere between the two nuances of body and mind is an avenue where the two can meet and find recognition and acceptance of each other. This is true alchemy and what You, my Soul, wishes to enlighten me to.

This is what You are showing me, as the softer I become, the louder You speak. The more open I am, the more You reveal to me. So, show me and guide me. I am waiting in earnest.

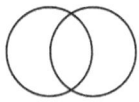

Love Letter Nineteen
Soul Grows Character

Dear Beloved

You say:
Character does not grow Soul.
Soul grows character.
   At first, I do not understand You. It is confusing to know that who I have been is not who You are or who You are asking me to be. I have been living as a projection of what my mind has deemed appropriate to enable me to live in a state of mediocrity within the confines of society. Until now I have hidden You, stashed You away, silenced You, and in turn dimmed my own light so I could remain anonymous and acceptable.
   I was brought up in a world where I was told that I need to DO something to BE someone. So, I applied my-

self to enhance all my greatest skills and strengthen my natural abilities as that would ensure that I became the best of who I could be. But I was seeking a pursuit that could not fill the gap in my heart.

It appeared on the outside at least that I had it all. My life was perfect, and I lived in paradise. But I knew the truth: that it was nothing more than a beautiful lie I hoped no-one else could see through.

It was not until You took me by the hand and asked me to look deeper. To dig down and find what I had hidden away. For that was the pain that was causing cracks on my surface. By not acknowledging the rumblings of bubbling lava buried beneath, it threatened to blow my whole cover at any minute. The more downwards pressure I applied to keep my secrets hidden, the more they pushed back with equal and opposing intensity.

I did not allow them to rise. Though one day, they burst free when the pressure had become too much and they propelled themselves up, annihilating everything I thought was 'true' on the surface. When the surge had subsided and the river of fire had cleared all in its wake, the barren wasteland of my existence lay in front of me. I was not my character; I was not the life I had carved out.

You stepped upon the charred, scorned earth,
smiling, knowing.
From destruction
comes rebirth.
Nature shows us this.
But yet we fail to see
that beauty shrivels,
life dies,

and nothing is forever.
The embodiment of the whole
is blended in the light and dark.

I had focused too much on creating something that I was not. With each ignorant and forced step I took, the distance between You and I grew, and I only became more hollow. Only when the outside shook and crumbled from lack of authenticity could I become aware of You. I threw myself into the vast expansive space that lay between us, committed to return to the part of me that I had forgotten even existed.

All I had to do was surrender my life as I knew it.

I did not do it willingly, even though I had become so drained keeping up this act. Fighting against that which I longed to be free from. In breathlessness, I collapsed, exhausted of existing as my false self. I wanted to live as You; I sought to embody You as there was nothing left for me to become. You were the truth I had not dared to step towards. When I willingly chose to, something else happened. I broke character. The play I had been acting in was interrupted as I no longer wanted to be in this role I had been preparing my whole life for, as it lacked substance.

I did not look different from the outside
but I had shed a lifetime of
believable,
fabricated
lies.

I was finally ready to embrace all that I had denied and withheld and allow You to create my being. You create what is real, what is honest, what is genuine – and that can be felt. It is not flimsy. It is not fake.

I am not the projected image my mind had created of me, I am not that human character, I am something even more than that. I had to drop the idea of who and what I thought I was to turn around and see the bigger opportunity of who I could be, and then still not even be attached to that.

When I cover You with my plans, my intentions and my expectations, I am seeking to control the wisdom and guidance You so freely wish to share, and manipulate it for my own egoic purposes. I veil You with my perceptions and dreams of a grander narrative.

Won't You teach me how to just be? To live in Your grace and be open to understand Your directive of perfect timing.

To be with all I am and all I am not now?

Please show me,

as I still have much to learn.

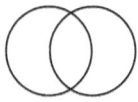

Love Letter Twenty
The Shadowlands

Dear Beloved

There is a mischievous irony You cast that never ceases to amaze me. I am mystified at how there can be so much joy in the demise and destruction of all that was false as that was the barrier preventing me from being free. The structures I'd built to uphold my life of prominence and ensure my envisioned success have collapsed.

It is remarkable that after a period of time, when the haze has cleared, how I can be so overwhelmingly grateful for the implosion that reduced to rubble the life I had been upholding. This has cracked my heart open to love more deeply and cry exuberant tears of joy at how free I feel when dancing on the burial ground of my former life. How is this possible?

Nothing seems to be left, and what has replaced it is expansive interdependence because inwardly my focus is now directed towards You. Not in the form of expectation and reliance upon You to do it all but in the trust and knowing that together we carry this load. Maybe it is delusion, maybe I am blinded by denial, but nothing compares to how open I feel when I create boundaries and support myself instead of putting everyone else before me.

Because I MATTER!
YOU MATTER!
WE MATTER!

I am done with playing small. No longer do I want to put all of my hopes and dreams aside or pour them halfheartedly into fruitless pursuits. I am willing, I am ready to live by following this inner truth. To adhere to listening to the call that is beckoning me to follow it. To trust when I've been diverted and shift gracefully when circumstances steer me in a different direction. To consciously release all I had believed would last forever. It is then that a sacred calm enfolds me. It is a peacefulness I have never known as liberation settles to make a home within me.

Sometimes the dark and mysterious unknown seems so threatening that all I want to do is crawl back to before. To try and cram myself into something I have outgrown. Because it is familiar. Because it is safe. Because it is known. But the intoxicating draw to what cannot be seen, felt or even comprehended, is stronger than the dread that can occasionally destabilise me.

There are times when all I want is the darkness in front of me, the vast openness of all that is yet unmanifested and pregnant with potential. There is so many opportunities eagerly awaiting my arrival because these energies want to engage me and remake me anew, but at times I am so hesitant, afraid I will die….

But that is the point.
Nothing will be the same
when you enter The Shadowlands.
For YOU,
my Beloved,
will step forward to claim me.
Showing me
that freedom
is the gift of the broken.

In one of the holiest cities in the world, Varanasi, death and life are inextricably entwined. Daily, bodies are ceremoniously placed upon the funeral pyre in reverence and honour of a life well lived. This is a final act of dissolution, a blessing to become free from the wheel of karma.

Therefore, to still be alive and witness myself cast off all I had known and all I had hoped to be, is to offer the veil of illusion that had distorted my true vision into those flames; to surrender the heavy burden I had carried and clung to fearfully. For it had been my security blanket, my safety, my identity. I let it go now for it has served its purpose, and I refocus so I can feel the lightness of BEing. Not DOing. Not expecting.

Just here, present now.
In all the unknowingness
and freedom of the broken.
More layers,
more layers,
more layers dissolve, until YOU are all that remains.

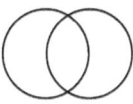

Love Letter Twenty-one
Accountability

Dear Beloved

Just when I think I have arisen from the depths, You confront me with another story I've created that needs to be examined and addressed. More and more inconsistencies You reveal to me. Faster and faster am I undressing myself of the beliefs, ideas and assumptions I'd deemed as certainty. I hadn't bothered to locate their origin once I'd found them caught in the net of my being. I hadn't examined closely to discover if they weren't lies I'd bought into. That is until now.

How many veils do I hide behind that keep 'me' from living and acting in the world as You?

How often do I unconsciously reach for those layers and pull the illusions back over me when I feel too exposed and vulnerable? I do it to be accepted. I do it so I can blend in with those who are around me so I don't stand out. For as much as I want to be free, I realise, I want to be captive too. It is easier to be on the inside looking out at what I believe the world has withheld from me, rather than seeing that I am in fact, outside, free to choose. It is easier to cast blame and not hold myself accountable when I believe it's everyone else's fault for my shortcomings. I have created the cage as much as I have the circumstances that hold me there.

I fight again the bars
that keep me in my place.
Though I forget that I am the builder
as well as the animal encaged.

I thought I had confronted death so many times that there were no more deaths to experience. I arrogantly believed I had reached a level of detachment. I asked You to show me the truth, to reveal to me what lay behind my disguises. Yet, I am still discerning which ones I want You to free me from. I invite You to liberate me from ones that feel restrictive, but not from ones that bring comfort, okay? As I still find some a security, not a burden. So, can you please leave this one intact?

No.
No special requests.
No favours.
No exceptions.
Place your trust in Me and be free.
Freedom is not restricted
to only your burdens,
it encases your desires too.

Lay down your arms and
end the war of keeping your image,
your face,
your idea and belief of who you think you are
and see what rises up
when all that was false
has been pulled down.

The freedom You speak of, my Beloved, comes at a price and that is one of ignorance. No longer can I play the fool and act dumb. You have stripped me of the belief that reaching solely for sensory fulfilment and luxurious offerings will vanquish the emptiness I feel. They are pleasing and can momentarily fill the void and the hole in my heart, but ultimately, I remain unsatisfied. What has kept me satiated in the past is dull and insipid now.

What I am craving is substance, that which comes from a life enriched with meaning, even if it's just for me. I can no longer submit myself to act in way that will appease my parents, my partner, my children, my family, my friends, my colleagues, those who held expectations of me or those who couldn't really care less. To simply now choose that which ignites the spark in me as that is what opens the channel to You.

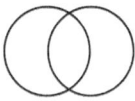

Love Letter Twenty-two
A Play of Shadow & Light

Dear Beloved

It all comes back to energetic frequency, does it not?

When in harmony, I pull in that which I am emitting. My internal energetic charge creates the external landscape and whatever and whoever vibrates on that same frequency is drawn back to me.

Yet, when I have lost connection with You and my true nature, I slide down one side of the internal scale. Meekness, self-sabotage and unworthiness set in as there is no longer union with You to pacify me. I begin to question everything and I again feel alone in the world, ill-equipped and unprepared to embody that which is greater than me.

This is when I am most vulnerable. If I am not paying close attention to discover the wounded aspect playing out in me as well as the shadow that seeks to hide it, does the world act accordingly and make manifest this drama so I can comprehend it with my own eyes. A veritable physical experience to the one that is occurring within. Figures I perceive as grandiose, arrogant and self-servicing are paraded in front of me, to highlight the shadows that are my own. As I am the source, so too am I the magnet. This internal frequency sets the tone for how my life will unfold. The deeper inward I go and the more I uncover what needs my attention, my love, my understanding and forgiveness, the more I can offer this grace to the world.

I have seen and experienced many times someone I simply 'click' with. Someone who gets me instantly and I think 'ah…they know'. They too have met YOU. They too are in connection with their Soul and have embarked upon The Journey Divine. There are other people I meet who I am certain are not yet aware of the richness that awaits them when they turn to You, as the unspoken language that is in wordless dialogue between us goes unnoticed. Their inner ear is as yet untuned to the silent echo calling to them from within. One day they may find, when they reach back into their shadow, that You are the one guiding them.

> We are blinded
> by a veil
> we cannot see,
> yet
> covers us all.
> We have forgotten
> our roots,
> our selves,

our souls.
Only by removing
all that is in our sight,
all that we believe
ourselves to be,
can we again perceive
the world
from the place
that knows.

The more I tune into You the clearer the messages return to me. Only in the thunderous cacophony of silence can I hear, when I sit inside and listen. All the knowledge and wisdom that books provide is incomparable to what lays inside. I can make myself smarter and read and read and read but those same printed words of the wise will only be taken in when I am ready to hear.

The trick is to get out of my head and dissolve back into all that is around me. To sense flesh and body merging with all that is – the frayed edges of my being entwining with the earth that is reaching out to touch me, to teach me. It matters not if anyone else can understand what is directing my course, so long as it makes sense to me to trust in the guidance of an unseen hand and be moved by an unseen force.

Signs are the language of Soul and show up as small intricacies in the universal order of things. With an open heart they are easy to decipher as their appearance is purely personal. For whilst Spirit is universal, Soul is personal. You, my Beloved, are the middleman in the interplay of life. Everyone wants to connect to Source, to be in the light, but most forget about You. They forget about their own personal Soul, as light appears to be the thing most desired. Light over darkness. You are the way to connection as well as the way to embodiment.

You cannot remain in heaven.
At some point
Hell will invite you to journey
to the centre of yourself
and all you have known
will come undone
in a flash
and you will see…as you have not seen before.

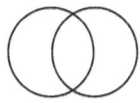

Love Letter Twenty-three
Overcoming Resistance

Dear Beloved

At times I find myself holding back, lagging and procrastinating as the elaborate disguise of self-sabotage entices me yet again. Seducing me away from what is calling me to take action. I can make a million and one excuses as to why I cannot/should not/will not apply myself at this very moment to the thing I know will be of benefit to me.
    I am not ready.
    I have no inspiration.
    I do not feel like it.
    Where do I even begin?
    Washing and cleaning and eating
    are more important.
    And they all seem

very logical and reasonable.
I am so good at acting
that at times I fool myself.
But I cannot fool You.

You wait patiently as You know I have to be more devoted in love than the resistance holding me hostage and keeping me small through fear. Completion of any task only comes with persistence – with a commitment to show up and move forward regardless of circumstance or waiting for the pleasure of 'feeling' like it. Yet, I am beginning to understand motivation is an impulse charged by the current of love, manifesting as devotion. It is the ability to intentionally step towards that which fosters growth and improvement by choosing an action. The action returns me to my true nature and offers expansion over that which confines me and causes separation from it. Having the whip cracked over me in the past, either by my own mind or from others seeking to improve me, has only left me defiant, causing a revolt and complete insubordination to authority.

When I tune into You, Your understanding, forgiveness and empathy encourage me as You offer me grace. In order to shift, I have to become aware that this stuckness I'm perceiving is coming from a lack of love for myself and is only perpetuating my idea of powerlessness, limiting my capacity to become fully immersed in life. This is when You step back, for You know I have to choose this for me, out of devotion to Self, no longer because I should.

It is a slow plod to inch my way towards that which I want, towards that which I believe is going to serve the greatest good for all as well as me. Years of dedicated effort with little to show at the surface might be all that unfolds, yet pulsing beneath there is a vast new network of potential, power and radiance. Others may not see it, I may not even see it, but there is a transformation taking place within.

Occasionally, I become internally disorientated and again fall under the hypnotic trance my mind weaves, manipulating me into believing who I 'should be' as opposed to who I 'could be' that prevents me from taking even a single step forward. Practicality and responsibility again cast their doubts and overshadow Your subtle guidance. Those gnarly voices inside keep taunting me, but they are the same ones that really only want to keep me safe from a fate I have projected, A fate worse than death: Dishonour.

I fear
that by speaking,
that by sharing my voice,
offering my craft,
and honouring my gift,
my life and
my Soul
will not only be silenced
but worse,
condemned.
For simply
showing up
and being
authentically
me.
So, I stay
silent.

And safe.

But empty.

And dying in the wake
of my own crippling
self-doubt.

The paralysing fear that disables me and renders me incapacitated is all consuming. The looming oppressive threat of never being good enough to be heard/seen/acknowledged, enfolds me, strangling me in its clutches. The more I fight it, the tighter its hold on me. It restricts my movement and keeps me small.

For too long I have fought the clutches of this unseen force; I have let it squeeze the life and all my creative juices out of me. It has exhausted me and prevented me from stepping into the embodiment of who I could be. Even when I take a moment to stop and catch my breath, the grip tightens and my ability to regain that lost ground is even more challenging.

But now I surrender. Not as a lifeless shell that lays defeated in the hands of an unseen force wanting to disempower me, but to the idea of perfection that has been constricting me. I now see the only way to free myself from that tight bind is to recognise my humanity. I am both fallible and divine, an awkward combination thrust into a melting pot with other beings who are all struggling to integrate the same.

No longer does my own self-doubt require feeding, further diminishing my own self-worth. Instead, I choose to fill myself with pride, determined to change my life's course through the small steps I can take right now. As I do, I move into You, the greater part of myself, which loosens the grip of fear.

    No longer am I pushing from the inside out.
I am naturally growing and moving the borders
of my body, my mind, my reality
with a focused effort
of simply doing
that which makes me feel whole.
Without recognition
or validation.
Without any other reason
than to show up
and do this
simply
for me.

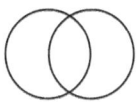

Love Letter Twenty-four
The True Depth of Love

Dear Beloved

I jump the fence of reality, climbing over the weathered railings into the field where You stand. You constantly await my awareness to be turned in Your direction. You are my personal guide in this wide expanse that can be found within and that opens to beingness, knowingness and love. In the meadows beyond my mind, I return to being free.

    When the chaos of life gets too much, when the outside world gets too loud and overbearing, I draw down the blinds of my eyes, close the curtains of my world and turn back into You. Back into the darkness, back into expansion, back into the sacred space of oneness, the sanctuary where You and I converge. No-one can touch it, no-one can reach it, for it is a hidden grotto purely for You and I. The world outside can grow and expand me, but it will hold no true value if I have not found it already within.

I am of the world
but not bound to it.
I can dip in
and move out
with ease,
with free will.
When I'm out of alignment,
I turn in
to recentre,
to gain strength
and drink
from the fountain
of knowledge
that flows freely within.
The cool waters of Soul
revitalising my being
and returning me to peace
so that again I can move forward.
My heart leading the way
into all that is
yet unknown
but ripe
with potential.

But still there is a desire to find union, my senses wanting to be placated through form. To find that deep connection that I am building with You, my Beloved, manifested in the body of another. To feel delicate fingertips caressing the small of my back, or hear words of affection being breathed into my ear. To be intoxicated and aroused by the smell of another and taste the joy when lips connect. How can I satisfy this desire of yearning to open to love yet not lose myself in the process?

Radiate from within and all is drawn to you, I hear You say.
Turn up the volume of your own light.
Amplify, expand and grow.
Be your own succulent, juicy delight
and more of the world will you know.
Pour yourself into yourself
so you can know
the true depth
of love.

Only when I have embodied the love that I experience with You, my Beloved, where I am loved without conditions, hesitations, restrictions or reservations do You show me I can truly love another. Any distortion of this experience I encounter internally will appear before me externally.

In wanting to turn outwards to have my feelings of love validated do I recognise this as proof that I am still not completely comfortable in holding them within. There is an uneasiness in my emotions that I seek to have warranted, compounding me with a sense of lack, that somehow I am missing out.

You show me I have to till the soil and prepare the ground of my own being before planting anything of value I want to grow in my life. This takes time, especially when the field has been unattended, unkept and unloved for years. Patience is required to make ready the soil and all I am doing now – clearing the debris of my past and my infertile aspects that smother life instead of encouraging it will only enhance my potential to yield a success crop.

My healing is what needs to take precedence. Our connection must be the priority.

Then, when I finally can see the value in me, will I refrain from surrendering myself for another.

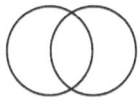

Love Letter Twenty-five
Receptivity

Dear Beloved

Sometimes You are the one driving the dream, and sometimes the dream is the only thing that drives me. Small incremental steps so often appear to lead nowhere, that this path of life I am plodding along only takes me further into limbo and perhaps even backwards. When I look to the horizon of all I wish to achieve, it feels that I have made little progress towards it despite the many steps I have taken. How can it be that the distance has not been closed? The gap seems only to have widened…

You have told me, shown me, taught me to not go so far out – to not grasp desirously for all I want. For then it only alludes me. The butterfly flies away and remains ever so illusively just out of my grasp. So, You tell me to wait and let it land on me.

BUT IT IS JUST THERE!
I CAN REACH OUT AND CAPTURE IT!

Let it come to you, You say.

And it would be so easy to do so. To lean over, to reach out, to catch a hold of the thing I so desperately want that appears just in front of me. But I am held from doing so as I'm learning to keep my energy intact.

Just be still and wait. Give it a chance to approach you. You do not have to hunt down and capture what you want. This is not your lesson now; it has been in the past, but not now. Your lesson is receptivity. To become aware of the magnet you are. Wisdom is held not in not doing, but applying yourself without an intended outcome. The secret is knowing the difference. It will come to you effortlessly when you have opened to all that you are. Not who you strive to be. No amount of pushing can make things happen faster, You assure me.

That minute gap, that space between stillness and action, intention and effort, pull and push, can appear so small but yet the entire universe can fit into it. The more I stretch and try to bridge the gap so as to hold what lies on the other side, the further away it becomes. No longer will force propel me towards that which I want for 'me', as trust now invites my attention to come and be still with it, as when I do, I see there's a 'we'. You tell me just to stay focused on what I am creating as that is the frequency I'm sending out, which all of life is listening to. You ask me to hand over control because when I return it to You do I remember how much easier life becomes.

It is taking every ounce of my strength to do so, when what feels most natural is to leap and throw myself into that chasm and onto 'that' thing with feverish ardour. Like a racehorse in the barriers, nervous with excitement and an eagerness to run, to chase and gallop towards the finish, you keep holding me back. You open the barrier and tell me to hold myself back.

I see the flying tails of all those in front of me, hurling towards their future, towards their dreams, and yet you tell me to hold. It is useless and demoralising to compare my progress to others as their journeys are not my own. Their outlines become distant figures that bask in the glow of the setting sun and yet I see nothing coming my way.

All is seen in the light.
It is the darkness
that you stand before
which holds within it
all that you seek,
all that you want,
all you desire.
The unknown holds gifts
more bountiful that you imagine.
So, wait.
It is coming to find you.
And take you
and love you,
and give you more
than you could possibly
imagine.
Hold and wait.

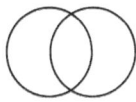

Love Letter Twenty-six
The Return

Dear Beloved

I think I can now begin to perceive where You have been leading me. Over the highest of mountains and down the steepest of ravines, though the deepest of valleys and the thickest of trees, to this space now before me, where the forest thins out and the sky can open wide. In the centre a solitary figure, one familiar to the eye, stokes a fire at the centre of an enclosed circle. Time may have knitted itself around those limbs and bones but the lines hold the memories and wisdom from the stories I have lived. You beckon me to join, to sit by the flames and to allow the remembrance to come to me. This ancient and sacred aspect has been waiting for my return. Waiting, to be reunited. Waiting. Peacefully and patiently, in the infiniteness of time.

'How long have you been waiting for me?' I ask.

Since the very beginning.

This was the final place I needed to come to regain that which I did not realise was missing. In the most remote, neglected and desolate region of my shadowlands, to find that which had been forgotten.

To get here I had relied upon intuition, guided by an unseen and unknown hand, one that reached out to me from beyond, connecting and realigning me with all that I was. That was You, my Beloved. Bit by bit, you had called me home. Only ever giving me as much as I could grasp at once. I had to be spoon-fed the knowingness – too much and I'd only end up doubting and rejecting. Every time I edged closer to You, Your invitation only grew more compelling.

Return to this world of which you belong.

'Why have You waited for me here in this place? In the darkness? All alone?' I wanted to know.

This is where you left me...

You have remained unseen and hidden away in the deepest recesses of the wild inside. To reach You, this innate part of me, had meant taking the longest journey of which I had been reluctant to embark. Fear could easily have kept me rooted living a domesticated, decent life, though I chose to disrobe myself of everything I had been to go in search for what is not easily found. I had to surrender my life and be prepared to lose it all to regain this vital last piece, as this was where the treasure lay. I had to give up everything that was attached to the old me so as to rebirth and bring this piece back up to the surface and embody it into the world.

If I ask You to come, will You follow?
To merge with the light and be free?
Will You cross the bridge of separation?
So that united, we can live in harmony?

Shrouded and hidden underneath, yet woven into the fabric that constituted all my pain, all my joy, all my exterior projections and my internal dialogue, You have waited. At the bottom of my sadness. In the middle of my uncertainty. At the height of my elation. You felt me getting closer and waited. All You had to do was amplify Your vibration so that I felt you more than the emotion I was feeling, and I was naturally magnetised to You. No grasping, no seeking, no pulling at me to come to You. You let me return in my own time, for You knew I always would.

I cannot demand that You come with me as a prized capture of my enduring journey, but I wish for You to join me, in the realms of life. I desire for You to return with me to the land that I know. For You are the one who I want to live there with me. You are the one who will help me to grow, to expand and to evolve.

I cannot go any further on my journey if You decline my offer, as a fractured part will always remain in the darkness. So, I will stay here with You until You are ready to return. I will not leave You as I have before.

But this is what I have been waiting for. Now it is time. There is much work to do...

By reclaiming my own Soul, this land of shadow is no longer scary, foreign or uncomfortable, for I am now illuminated, having activated the light that waited inert in the darkness of my own ignorance. To walk back is a homecoming; to retrace steps that took my malnourished form, starved of divinity from the world I knew, but to now re-enter it buoyant, enamoured and in union. No longer searching, no longer broken. Whole. Connected through Soul.

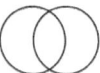

To reclaim one's Soul in a world that has ensured we disembody it is our main task, and one that is not for the faint of heart. But if you seek, so you shall find, and the life you have known will never be the same again. There is a part of you that has been regained and reunited, which no-one and nothing can ever claim from you. It is yours; it is you. Your Soul wants to be with you as much as you want to be with it. If you cannot hear, feel or sense your Soul, I invite you to turn around inside yourself and be courageous, calling out lovingly into your shadow:

> Dear beloved,
> I am yours,
> now and always.
> Guide me,
> ever,
> on.

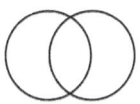

Love Letter Twenty-seven
Integration

Dear Beloved

Is it possible that we have come to a point in the journey where everything has been leading? To be with You and be reborn back into this life in a completely different form. To have come undone and lost everything that was associated with my outer body character rather than my inner Soul landscape.

All the attachments, binds, mentality and association with that persona, with that act, have now been stripped away. The show is over, the lights have dimmed and the figure left in the darkness is me. No longer do the lights from the outside blaze to create illumination so I can be seen. I now generate my glow to light up the world around me. I see that it is You, my Soul, my Beloved who makes me shine. When I embody You, no force outside of me can generate as much power as what I have within.

I can now see how every single moment of my life has led me here. To this point. I have been slowly unravelling for years, but yet I have not seen. Things have fallen apart and away quicker and faster. All that has not served me has been severed at lightning speed, even when I wanted it. Even when I believed THAT was the thing that was going to make me MAKE IT. Or be whole. Or be someone. With haste, You abruptly undressed me of all these external things – these outfits of desire and dress-ups of falsehoods that fooled only me.

Every single person has been some pebble that has lined the way of my journey to this point. With clarity I see all my broken relationships. All the pain of my shattered heart and the fractured shards of my ego have occurred for a reason. They have been left behind in those frozen moments of time, waiting for me to return and embrace them. Now that I have gathered them up and offered compassion, understanding, love, forgiveness and acceptance to them, I have regained those 'lost' pieces of myself. I have welcomed them in, bidding them to return to the land of the living with me and no longer remain in the pain of the past. Now, I find that I am whole.

No-one could save me but myself.
I had to be my own hero.
Ride in gallantly,
on my white horse
and scoop myself up.
And carry the forgotten,
the hurt,

the abandoned,
the betrayed,
the shamed,
part of me
back.
To now.
To collect it from the shadow
and bring it
to this present moment in time.
Rebirth it into my physical body.
Because that is how much I love You.
For to leave YOU, a piece of me,
in a place that is not now
is to become hollow and empty.
Void of Soul.
And only when
all these fractured parts are returned
can I really be free from the past,
to live embodied
with all my divinely cracked pieces
remoulded
in a collage of love and unity.

And now here we stand, at the dawn of a new emergence of Soul. Of You. To embody me. And me to fully embody You. No more barriers, no more walls, no more restrictions, reservations or dismissals. The time is now, for when I embody You, I encourage all those around me to proudly step forward and do the same.

A revolution is approaching, and it is one of love. It is where we love ourselves and no longer search for someone else to fill that cup up for us. To really and truly merge with who we are. SOUL. And what You have always called us to be. To return to our bodies, to return to our lives having reclaimed the wounds of our past as our medals of honour.

To tell our stories with pride, sharing the tales of the heroes that we are by reclaiming our own Soul. How we are the ones victorious. For we are those who have remembered. We are no longer a victim of circumstance for we understand that we are conscious directors creating roleplays so as to extend ourselves to even greater capacities.

For not only are we the actor, but we have also written the script of our lives in union with our Soul for our greatest learning. When we realise we are playing our own story, the one that has been penned by our own hand, then we too can change the outcome and become triumphant in the narrative of our lives.

YOU, my Beloved, smile at my remembrance of all I have been, and distinctly because of who I am. Which is You.

More are coming this way…

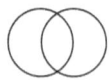

The Offering

That is why YOU are here, dear reader. I hold up the torch for you, in the darkness. Keep walking, keep walking. Soon you will see and be reminded of who you are. The You without effort. The You that simply is. The road may be long, but trust. For Soul has you. As it has me. And when you connect to Soul, you connect to the entire world and all that is found within it. Return and be free.

Know too, that all is within you. You have it all, just give yourself the space to naturally unfold. Say it aloud with me:

I am the vessel through which the Universe manifests.
My Soul is that of the Divine.
I am endless.
I am infinite.
I am love,
I am love,
I am love.

For you are and you always have been.
United we stand, and together we will rise.

I am yours, Beloved, now and always.
Guide me,
ever,
on.

ABOUT THE AUTHOR

Dare to let yourself sink deep into all that is unknown yet pregnant with potential by immersing yourself in the words of soulful storyteller, Alana Grainger.

Her approach is simple yet engaging: to call out to that expansive void within and be still and silent whilst awaiting for the truth to echo back. Her writing is not only sentimental in her lamentation for longing and union but empowering, as it provides the wisdom to reconcile life to one that is embodied and sovereign.

Alana Grainger speaks to those who are searching for something that cannot be easily found, yet can be deeply felt. Through her work, she weaves the narrative of Soul, inviting us to step boldly into authenticity and integrity by shedding the masks that hold us back. Passionate about uncovering the hidden treasures and dormant gifts within, she gently guides others through the exploration of darkness and shadow, knowing that true strength is not in how much we can endure, but in how much we can open.

Her wisdom comes from lived experience and personal evolution: a certified yoga teacher, healer and visionary, having lived in the sacred lands of India and Bali where she discovered that survival is not about holding it all together, but when it falls apart, that there is a love that will catch you and has been waiting, patiently, for you to come home.

Enjoyed the book? You can follow Alana Grainger at:

Website: alanagrainger.com
Instagram: alana_grainger
Facebook: alana.grainger82
Email: alanagrainger@gmail.com

If you enjoyed the book, please leave a review on Amazon, Goodreads or with the author directly. Reviews are invaluable in supporting an author's work and are much appreciated.

www.ingramcontent.com/pod-product-compliance
Lightning Source LLC
Chambersburg PA
CBHW060402080526
44583CB00012B/432